Time for Bed!

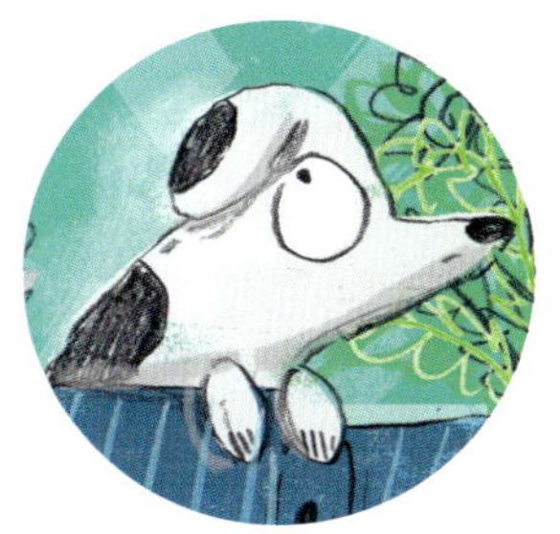

Written by
Stephen Rickard

Illustrated by
Pauline Reeves

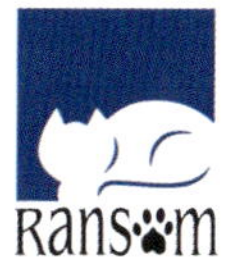

Ransom

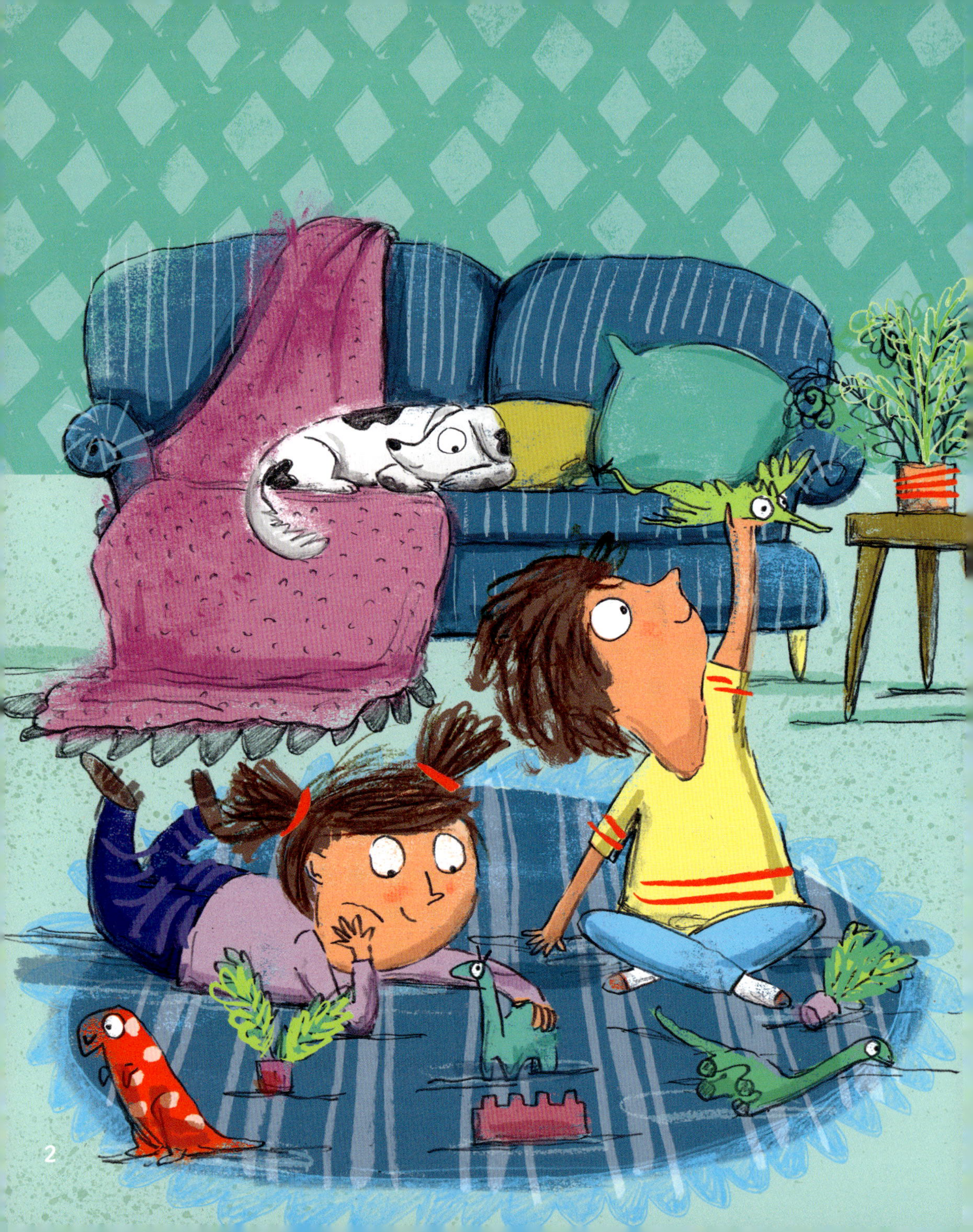

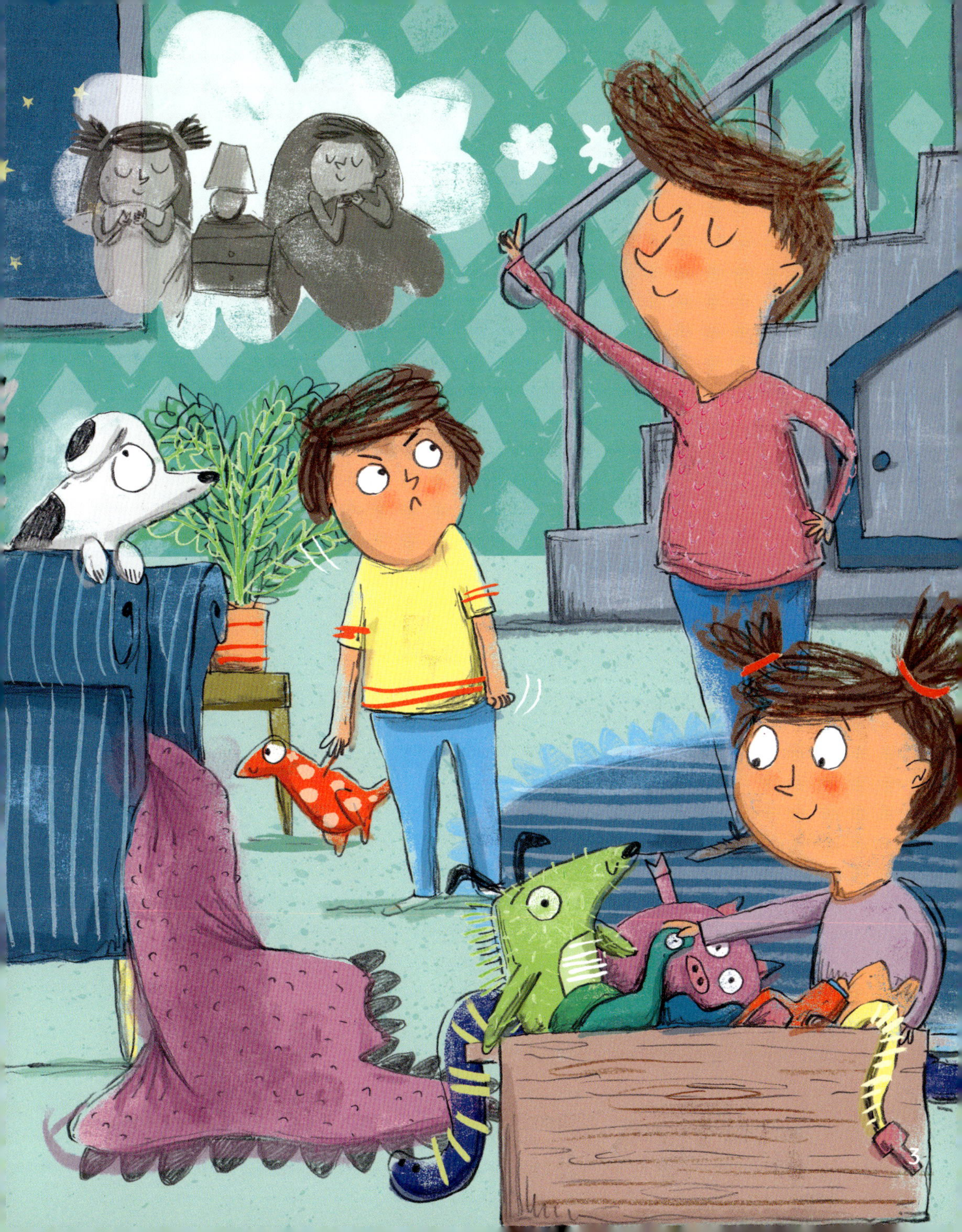

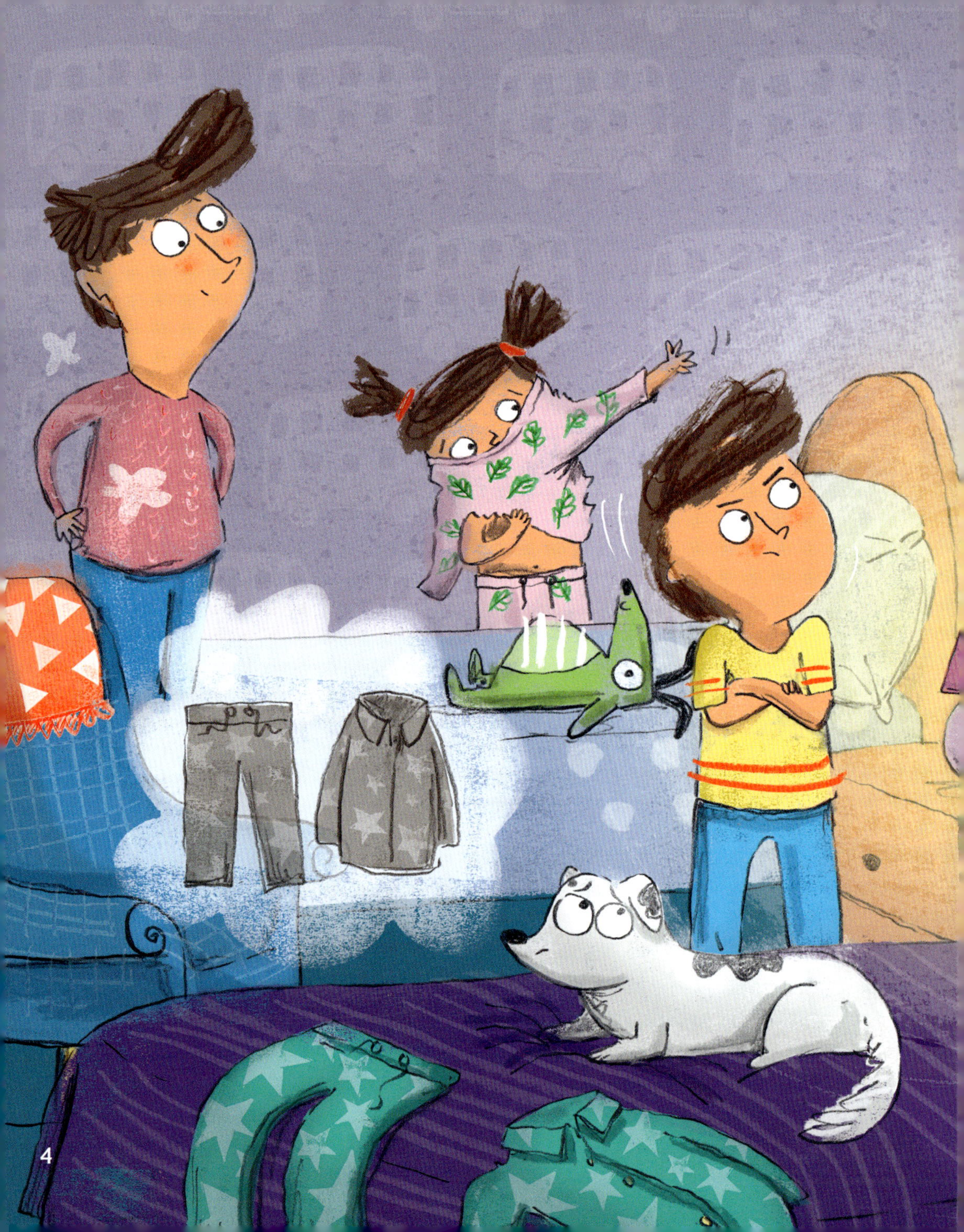

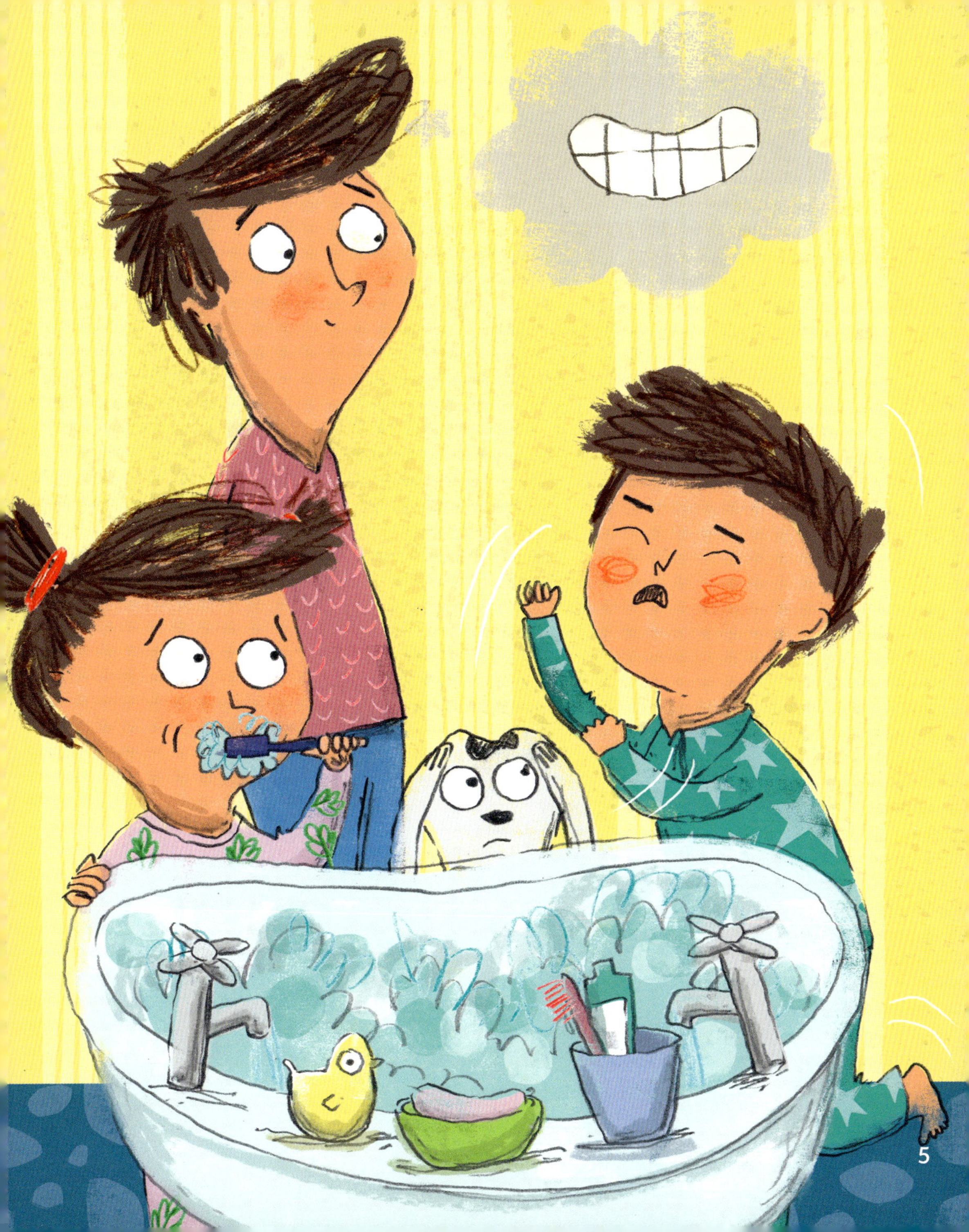

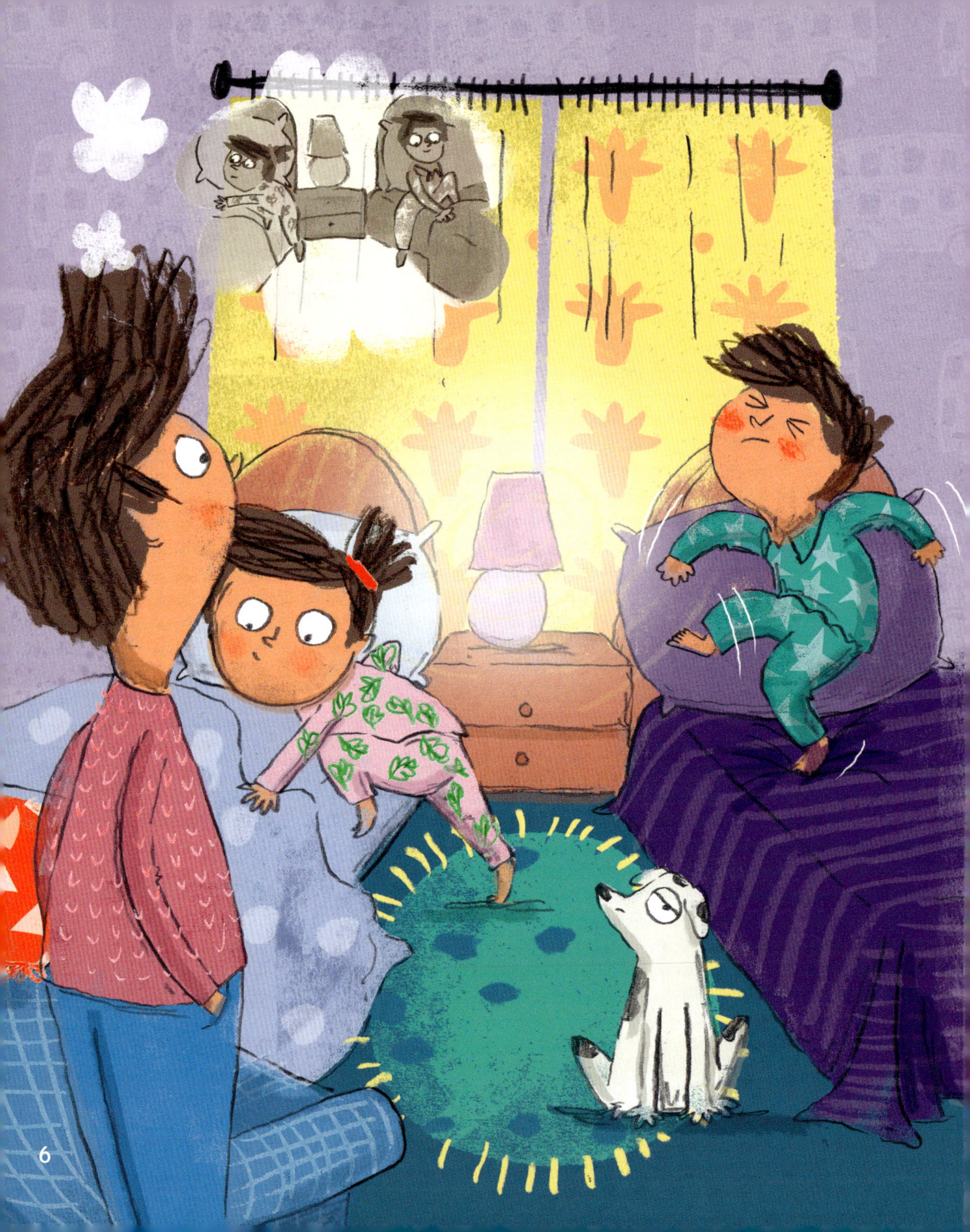

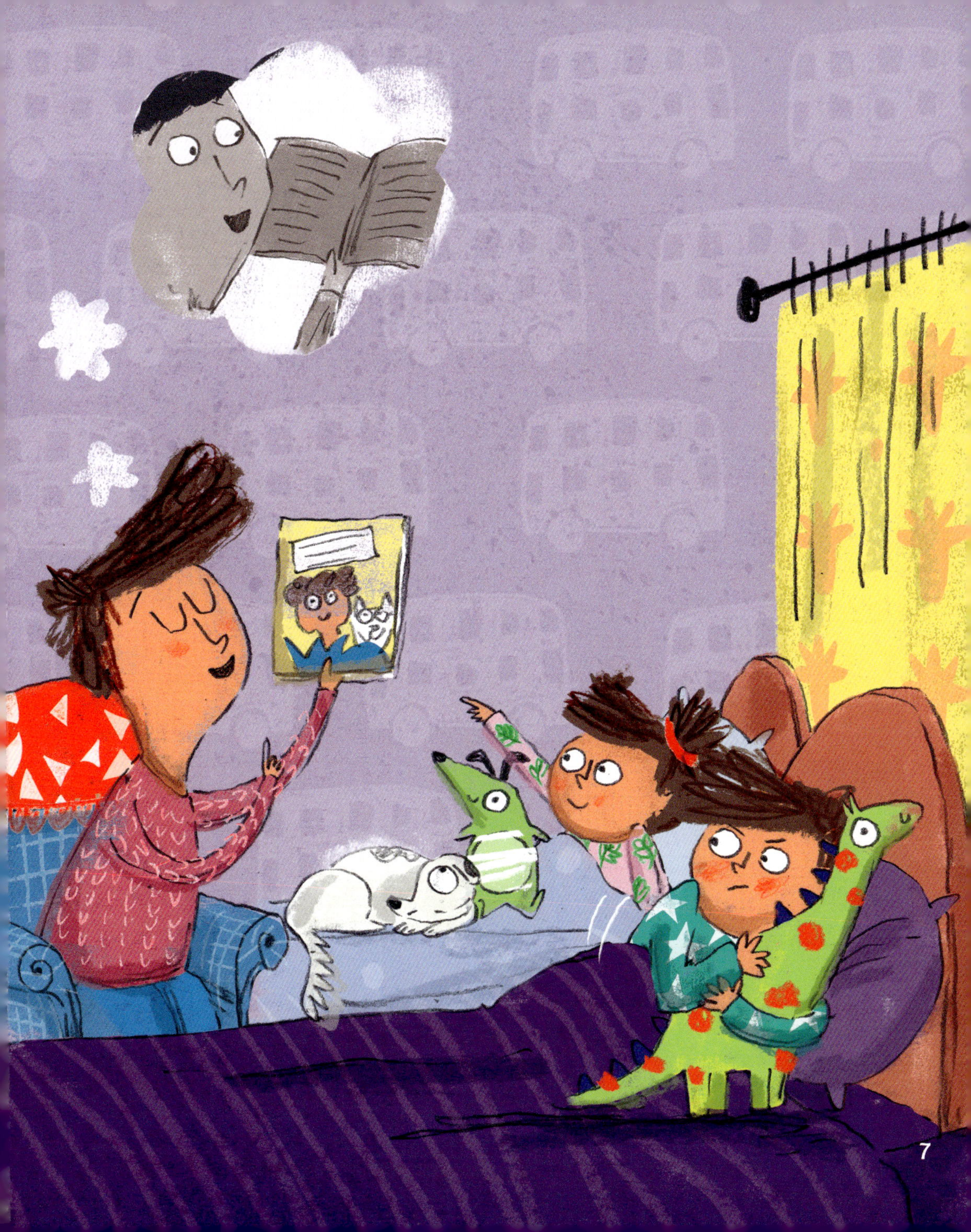

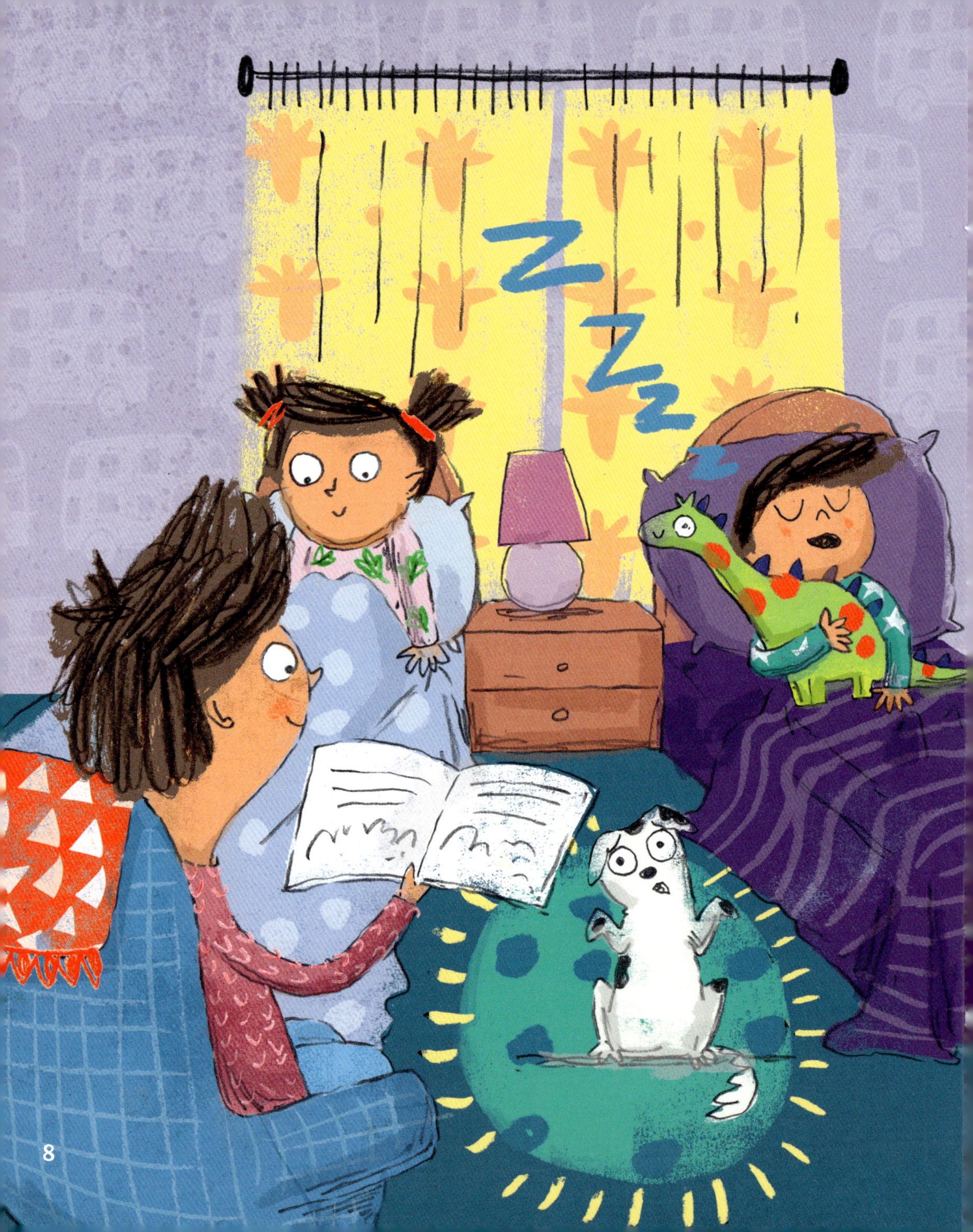